Lecture Outlines for Note T

for

Atkinson and Hilgard's

Introduction to Psychology
Fourteenth Edition

Australia • Canada • Mexico • Singapore • Spain • United Kingdom • United States

Printed in the United States of America
2 3 4 5 6 7 06 05 04 03

Printer: Patterson Printing Company

0-534-58634-1

For more information about our products,
contact us at:
Thomson Learning Academic Resource Center
1-800-423-0563

For permission to use material from this text,
contact us by:
Phone: 1-800-730-2214
Fax: 1-800-731-2215
Web: http://www.thomsonrights.com

Asia
Thomson Learning
5 Shenton Way #01-01
UIC Building
Singapore 068808

Australia/New Zealand
Thomson Learning
102 Dodds Street
Southbank, Victoria 3006
Australia

Canada
Nelson
1120 Birchmount Road
Toronto, Ontario M1K 5G4
Canada

Europe/Middle East/South Africa
Thomson Learning
High Holborn House
50/51 Bedford Row
London WC1R 4LR
United Kingdom

Latin America
Thomson Learning
Seneca, 53
Colonia Polanco
11560 Mexico D.F.
Mexico

Spain/Portugal
Paraninfo
Calle/Magallanes, 25
28015 Madrid, Spain

Table of Contents

Chapter	**Page**
Chapter 1: The Nature of Psychology	1
Chapter 2: Biological Foundations of Psychology	7
Chapter 3: Psychological Development	15
Chapter 4: Sensory Processes	19
Chapter 5: Perception	23
Chapter 6: Consciousness	29
Chapter 7: Learning and Conditioning	31
Chapter 8: Memory	35
Chapter 9: Language and Thought	41
Chapter 10: Motivation	45
Chapter 11: Emotion	51
Chapter 12: Intelligence	55
Chapter 13: Personality	57
Chapter 14: Stress, Health, and Coping	63
Chapter 15: Abnormal Psychology	67
Chapter 16: Treatment of Psychological Disorders	73
Chapter 17: Social Influence	77
Chapter 18: Social Cognition	81

Chapter 1: The Nature of Psychology

Psychology Defined
- The scientific study of behavior and mental processes

The Scope of Psychology
- Brain damage and face recognition (prosopagnosia)
- Attributing traits to people (attribution error)
- Childhood amnesia
- Obesity
- Media violence and children's aggression

The Historical Origins of Psychology
- Origins in Greek philosophy
- Famous Greek philosophers
  - Socrates
  - Plato
  - Aristotle

The Nature-Nurture Debate
- Are human capabilities inborn or acquired through experience?

The Nature View
- Humans enter the world with an inborn store of knowledge and understanding of reality

The Nurture View
- Knowledge is acquired through experience and interactions with the world
- John Locke – 17th century English philosopher – mind a *tabula rasa* or blank slate

The Beginnings of Scientific Psychology
- Wilhelm Wundt
  - University of Leipzig, Germany, 1879
  - First psychological laboratory
  - Introspection

Structuralism
- E.B. Titchener
  - Cornell University
  - Analysis of mental structures

Functionalism
- William James
  - Harvard University
  - Studied how the mind works to enable an organism to adapt to and function in its environment

Newer Schools of Psychology 1920's
- Behaviorism
- Gestalt
- Psychoanalysis

Behaviorism
- John B. Watson
  - All behavior is a result of conditioning
  - The environment shapes behavior by reinforcing specific habits

Gestalt Psychology
- Gestalt – German word meaning "form" or "configuration"
- Gestalt psychologists
  - Max Wertheimer, Kurt Koffka,Wolfgang Kohler
- Primary interests
  - Perception of form, motion, size, color
- Influences on modern social psychology

Psychoanalysis
- Sigmund Freud
- Psychoanalysis
  - Role of the unconscious
  - Method of free association
  - Dream analysis

Later Developments 20th Century Psychology
- Increased interest in psychology following WWII
- Expansion of theoretical approaches
  - Psycholinguistics
  - Neuropsychology
  - Cognitive Psychology

Contemporary Psychological Perspectives
- Biological perspective
- Behavioral perspective
- Cognitive perspective
- Psychoanalytic perspective
- Subjective perspective

The Biological Perspective
- Specifies the neurobiological processes that underlie behavior and mental processes
  - depression
  - face recognition
  - memory

The Behavioral Perspective
- Focuses on observable stimuli and responses
  - conditioning
  - reinforcement

The Cognitive Perspective
- Concerned with mental processes such as perceiving, remembering, reasoning, deciding, problem solving
  - information processing
  - memory

The Psychoanalytic Perspective
- Behavior stems from unconscious processes, including beliefs, fears and desires that a person is unaware of, but that still influence behavior

The Subjective Perspective
- Human behavior is a function of the perceived world, not the objective world
  - person's definition of the situation
  - stresses cultural and individual differences
  - effects of motivation and emotion

Major Subfields of Psychology
- Biological Psychology
- Experimental Psychology
- Developmental Psychology
- Social and Personality Psychology
- Clinical and Counseling Psychology
- School and Educational Psychology
- Organizational and Engineering Psychology

Biological Psychology
- Studies relationships between biological processes and behavior

Experimental Psychology
- Uses experimental methods to study how people and other animals react to sensory stimuli, perceive the world, learn and remember, reason and respond emotionally

Developmental Psychology
- Human development and the factors that shape behavior from birth to old age

Social and Personality Psychology
- Social Psychology
  - Interested in how people perceive and interpret their social world
  - How beliefs, emotions, behaviors are influenced by the real or imagined presence of others
- Personality Psychology
  - Studies the thoughts, emotions, behaviors of individuals
  - Studies the differences between individuals

Clinical and Counseling Psychology
- Clinical Psychology
  - Applies psychological principles to the diagnosis and treatment of emotional and behavioral problems, for example, mental illness, drug addiction, marital and family conflict
- Counseling Psychology
  - Studies emotional and behavioral problems of a less serious nature.
  - Frequently work with high school and university students

School and Educational Psychology
- School Psychology
  - Work with children to evaluate learning and emotional problems
- Educational Psychology
  - Specializes in learning and teaching. Work on research to improve teaching methods and train teachers

Organizational and Engineering Psychology

- Organizational Psychology
  - Involved with selecting people who are most suitable for particular jobs
- Engineering Psychology
  - Involved with improving human-machine interaction
  - Design machines for efficiency, better performance, safety and comfort

Psychological Research Terms

- Hypothesis
  - A statement that can be tested
- Theory
  - An interrelated set of propositions about a particular phenomenon
- Scientific
  - Unbiased
    - do not favor one hypothesis over another
  - Reliable
    - other qualified researchers can repeat the observations and obtain the same results
- Experiments
  - Investigator takes measurements under controlled conditions
- Variables
  - Independent Variable
    - "the hypothesized cause", under the control of the investigator
  - Dependent Variable
    - "the hypothesized effect", the outcome variable
- Experimental Groups
  - The group that receives the treatment
- Control Group
  - The group in which the hypothesized cause is absent
  - Used as a baseline against which the experimental group is compared
- Random Assignment
  - Each participant has an equal probability of being placed in any group
- Multivariate Experiments
  - Experimenters manipulate several independent variables at once

- Measurement
  - A system for assigning numbers to variables
    - Statistics
    - Mean
    - Statistically significant
- Correlation
  - Correlation coefficient
  - Positively correlated
  - Negatively correlated
  - Correlation and Causation
- Observation
  - Direct Observation
  - Survey Method
  - Case Histories
  - Literature Review

Ethics of Psychological Research
- Research with Humans
  - Minimal Risk
  - Informed Consent
  - Debriefing
  - Right to Privacy
- Research with Animals
  - APA guidelines
  - Federal guidelines

Chapter 2: Biological Foundations of Psychology

Neurons, The Building Blocks Of The Nervous System: Structure and Function

- Neurons
  - specialized cells that transmit neural impulses or messages to other neurons, glands and muscles
- Dendrites
  - short branch-like projections from the cell body which receive neural impulses from adjacent neurons
- Axon
  - a slender tube that extends from the cell body and transits messages to other neurons
- Synaptic terminals
  - tiny branches at the end of each axon that end in small swellings or buttons
- Synapse
  - a slight gap between the terminal button and the cell body. The gap itself is called the synaptic gap
- Neurotransmitter
  - a specialized chemical that diffuses across the synaptic gap and stimulates the next neuron
- Sensory neurons
  - transmit impulses received by receptors to the central nervous system
- Motor neurons
  - carry outgoing signals from the brain or spinal cord to muscles and glands
- Interneurons
  - receive the signals from the sensory neurons and send impulses to other interneurons or to motorneurons. Found only in the brain, eyes and spinal cord
- Nerve
  - a bundle of elongated axons belonging to hundreds or thousands of neurons
- Nucleus (nuclei)
  - a group of cell bodies of neurons in the brain and spinal cord
- Ganglion (ganglia)
  - a group of neuronal cell bodies found outside the brain and spinal cord

_____
_____
_____
_____
_____
_____
_____
_____
_____
_____
_____
_____
_____
_____
_____
_____
_____
_____
_____
_____
_____
_____
_____
_____
_____
_____

- Glial Cells
  - non-neural cells found in the nervous system, functioned to hold neurons in place, provide nutrients to neurons and maintain signaling capacity of neurons
- Action Potential
  - an electrochemical impulse that travels from the cell body down to the end of the axon
- Ion Channels
  - semi-permeable protein molecules that form pores across the cell membrane and regulate the flow of ions
- Resting membrane potential
  - the electrical potential of a neuron at rest
- Myelin Sheath
  - a sheath or coating consisting of specialized glial cells that wrap themselves around the axon
- All-or-none-principle
  - in response to any given synaptic input, a neuron either fires an action potential or it does not
- Excitatory neurotransmitters
  - allows positively charged ions to enter the neuron polarizing the receiving neuron and making the inside of the cell more positive than the outside
- Inhibitory neurotransmitters
  - allows positively charged ions to leave the neuron or negatively charged ions to enter the cell, thus making the inside of the receiving neuron more negative than the outside
- Reuptake
  - reabsorption of the neurotransmitter from the synaptic terminals from which it (the neurotransmitter) is released
- Degradation
  - The reaction of enzymes in a synaptic gap with the neurotransmitter, where it (the neurotransmitter) is broken down chemically and becomes inactive

Neurotransmitters
- More than 70 neurotransmitters have been identified
- Acetylcholine
  - usually excitatory, but can also be inhibitory
  - present in areas of forebrain called the hippocampus
  - prominent role in Alzheimer's disease
- Norepinephrine
  - Monoamine - class of neurotransmitters
  - present mainly in the brainstem
  - role in mood regulation
- Dopamine
  - Monoamine class of neurotransmitters
- Serotonin
  - Monoamine class of neurotransmitters
  - Role in mood regulation, role in depression (low levels)
  - Important in the regulation of sleep and appetite
- Glutamate
  - Role in schizophrenia (high levels) and Parkinson's disease (low levels)
  - Excitatory neurotransmitter
  - Present in more neurons of the CNS than any other neurotransmitter
  - Role in schizophrenia (disruption in glutamate transmission)
  - Role in memory formation
- GABA
  - Inhibitory neurotransmitter
  - Role in muscle movement
  - Anti-anxiety drugs enhance activity of GABA

The Organization of the Nervous System
Division of the Nervous System
- The central nervous system
  - all the neurons in the brain and spinal cord
- The peripheral nervous system
  - all the nerves connecting the brain and spinal cord to other parts of the body
- Somatic system
  - subdivision of the peripheral nervous system that carries messages to and from the sense receptors, muscles and the surface of the body

- Autonomic System
  - subdivision of the peripheral nervous system that connects with the internal organs and glands

The Organization of the Brain
- The hindbrain
  - all the structures located in the rear or posterior part of the brain closest to the spinal cord
- The midbrain
  - located in the middle of the brain
- The forebrain
  - all the structures located in the front or the anterior part of the brain

Structure and Function of the Brain
- Central core
  - regulates most primitive behaviors
- Limbic System
  - controls emotions
- Cerebrum
  - regulates our higher intellectual processes

Primary Areas
- The Primary Motor Area
  - controls voluntary movements of the body
- The Primary Somatosensory Area
  - produces sensory experiences, heat, cold, touch, pain, sense of bodily movement
- The Primary Visual Area
  - produces vision, interpretation of visual stimuli
- The Primary Auditory Area
  - analysis of complex auditory signals, particularly the temporal patterning of sound as in human speech
- Association Areas
  - primarily concerned with sensory or motor processes
    - Frontal association area
    - Role in memory and problem solving
    - Posterior association areas
    - Role in visual perception

Pictures of the Living Brain
- CAT or CT
  - computerized axial tomography
- MRI
  - magnetic resonance imaging
- PET
  - positron emission tomography

Asymmetries in the Brain
- Hemispheric differences in brain activity
- Broca's area (left hemisphere)
  - involved in speech production
- Split Brain Research
  - pioneering work of Roger Sperry

Hemispheric Specialization
- Left hemisphere
  - expressive language
  - logical activities
  - mathematical computation
- Right hemisphere
  - spatial and pattern recognition
  - facial identity and expressions of emotion
  - line slopes and dot locations

Language and the Brain
- Aphasia
  - language deficits caused by brain damage
- Expressive aphasia
  - damage to Broca's area
- Receptive aphasia
  - damage to Wernicke's area

The Autonomic Nervous System Two Divisions
- Sympathetic nervous system
  - active during times of intense arousal
- Parasympathetic nervous system
  - associated with rest

The Endocrine System
- Glands
  - organs located throughout the body that secrete special substances such as sweat, milk or particular hormones
- Hormones
  - chemicals secreted by the endocrine glands into the bloodstream and transported to other parts of the body

- Pituitary Gland
  - the "master gland", controls the secretion activity of other endocrine glands

Evolution, Genes and Behavior
- Natural selection
  - process described by Charles Darwin to account for evolutionary change
- Behavior genetics
  - combines the methods of genetics and psychology to study inheritance and behavioral characteristics

Evolution of Behavior
- Proximate causes of behavior
  - such as the firing of special motor neurons
- Ultimate causes
  - behavior in its evolutionary context
- Sexual selection
  - aspects of natural selection that yields traits that promote reproductive success

Chromosomes and Genes
- Genes
  - segments of deoxyribonucleic acid (DNA), molecules that form the fundamental hereditary unit
- Chromosomes
  - structure in the nucleus of each cell in the body. Most body cells contain 46 chromosomes: 23 from father's sperm, 23 from mother's ovum
- Dominant genes
  - individuals manifest traits specified by dominant gene
- Recessive genes
  - individuals manifest traits specified by recessive gene, if contributed by both parents

Genetic Studies and Behavior
- Selective breeding
  - animals that are high or low in a certain behavior or physical trait are mated with each other
- Twin studies
  - monozygotic, dizygotic twins
- Molecular genetics
  - influence of specific genes on personality, and other specific behavioral traits

- **Environmental influences on gene action**
  - role of environment and interaction in manifestation of a behavior or particular disorder

_____

_____

_____

_____

_____

_____

_____

_____

_____

_____

_____

_____

_____

_____

_____

_____

_____

_____

_____

_____

_____

_____

Chapter 3: Psychological Development

Nature and Nurture
- Nature-Nurture Debate
  - John Locke
    - "tabula rasa" or blank slate
- John Watson, B. F. Skinner (behaviorists)
- Interactionist approach
  - both nature and nurture

Stages of Development
- Maturation
  - an innately determined sequence of growth and change that is relatively independent of external events
- Stages
  - all children go through the same stages in the same order
  - behavior organized around a coherent theme or set of characteristics
- Critical Period
  - crucial time periods in a person's life when specific events occur if development is to proceed normally

Capacities of the Newborn
- Vision
  - Visual field- full scope of what can be seen
  - Facial preference- an inborn, unlearned preference for faces
- Hearing
  - Newborn infants can detect the different but very similar sound and can distinguish human voice and other kinds of sounds
- Taste and Smell
  - Preference for sweet-tasting liquids over liquids that are salty, bitter, sour or bland

Learning and Memory
- Important research findings for newborns
  - Memory in 3 month olds
  - Preference for human voices over other sounds
  - Preference of heartbeat sounds and mother's voice over other women's voices
  - Preference of familiar stories over unfamiliar stories

Cognitive Development in Childhood
Key Concepts
- Schemas
  - theories about how the physical and social worlds operate
- Assimilate
  - understand the world in terms of existing schema
- Accommodation
  - modify a schema to fit new information

Cognitive Development in Childhood
Piaget's Stages of Cognitive Development
- Sensorimotor (birth-2)
  - Object permanence
- Preoperational (2-7)
  - Conservation
  - Egocentrism
- Concrete operational (7-11)
- Formal Operational (11 and up)

Sociocultural Approaches
- Child should be seen as a newcomer to a culture, culture can influence children's development in several ways

Theory of Mind
- Metacognition
  - thinking about thinking
- Theory of Mind
  - study of children's knowledge about basic mental states such as desires, perceptions, beliefs, knowledge
- Study of Autism
  - a serious disorder in which children can seem unresponsive to others and tend to have significant problems communicating with others

Moral Development
- Leading Theorist
  - Lawrence Kohlberg
- Stages of moral reasoning
  - Preconventional
  - Conventional
  - Postconventional

Personality and Social Development
- Temperament
  - mood-related personality characteristics
- Pioneering research
  - Thomas and Chess
    - Easy temperament (1963)
    - Difficult temperament
    - Slow to warm up temperament

Attachment
- An infant's tendency to seek closeness to particular people and to feel more secure in their presence
- Pioneering research
  - Harlow (1969), Bowlby (1975)
    - Wire monkey versus terry cloth monkey

Attachment Research Findings
- Pioneering Research
  - Ainsworth (1958)
    - Securely attached
    - Insecurely attached - avoidant
    - Insecurely attached - ambivalent
  - Disorganized
- Sensitive responsiveness
  - response to baby's needs

Effects of Daycare
- Research findings
- Quality of day care

Gender Identity and Sex Typing
- Gender Identity
  - a firm sense of ourselves as either male or female
- Sex typing
  - acquisition of behavior and characteristics that a culture considers appropriate to one's sex

Gender Identity and Sex Type Theoretical Explanations
- Psychoanalytic Theory
  - phallic stage, oedipal conflict
- Social Learning Theory
  - emphasizes rewards and punishments
    - Observation
    - Learning
- Cognitive-Developmental Theory
  - gender identity develops slowly and then becomes stable

- Gender schema theory
  - a set of beliefs about gender- how self-concepts are organized

Adolescent Development
- The period of transition from childhood to adulthood
- Puberty
  - the period of sexual maturation biologically mature
- Menarche
  - the first menstrual period
- Psychological effects of puberty
  - implication of early vs. late maturation in girls and boys
- Identity development
  - Identity crisis
  - Identity confusion
- Stages of identity develop
  - James Marcia
    - Identity achievement
    - Identity foreclosure
    - Moratorium
    - Identity diffusion

Chapter 4: Sensory Processes

Characteristics of Sensory Modalities
- Sensitivity
  - sensory modalities at the psychological level
- Sensory coding
  - sensory modalities at a biological level
- Absolute threshold
  - the minimum magnitude of a stimulus that can be reliably discriminated from no stimulus at all

Characteristics of Sensory Modalities
- Psychophysical procedures
  - experimental techniques for measuring the relation between the physical magnitude of some stimulus and the resulting psychological response
- Psychophysical function
  - performance as a function of stimulus intensity
- Photon
  - the smallest unit of light energy

Characteristics of Sensory Modalities
- Standard
  - defined to be some arbitrary level and distinguished from the new, higher level
- Just noticeable difference (jnd)
  - the minimum difference in the stimulus magnitude necessary to tell two stimuli apart
- Leading researchers (19th century)
  - Ernst Heinrich Weber – physiologist
  - Gustav Fechner – physicist

Characteristics of Sensory Modalities
- Weber fraction
  - (proportional relation) by which the standard must be increased to be noticed is proportional to the intensity of the standard
- Suprathreshold conditions
  - conditions in which stimulus intensity is above threshold

_____

_____

_____

_____

_____

_____

_____

_____

_____

_____

_____

_____

_____

_____

_____

_____

_____

_____

_____

_____

_____

_____

_____

_____

_____

_____

Signal Detection Theory Defined
- A standard way of understanding how errors are made in many diverse situations

Signal Detection Theory Key Concepts
- Sensation
  - determined by the perceptual strength of the stimulus
- Bias
  - a criterion, set by the observer, for making a particular response
- Signal
  - what the observer is trying to detect
- Noise
  - anything in the environment irrelevant to what the observer is trying to detect

Hits and False Alarms
- Hit
  - a response of correctly responding yes when a signal is present
- False Alarm
  - a response of incorrectly responding yes when only noise is present
- Hit rate
  - the proportion of hits
- False alarm rate
  - the proportion of false alarms

Sensory Coding
- How stimuli are transmitted from the sensory receptors to the brain
- Transduction
  - translation of physical energy into electrical signals that can make their way to the brain, accomplished by specialized cells called receptors

Coding of Intensity and Quality Properties of any stimulus
- Intensity
  - the strength of the stimulus
- Quality
  - what the stimulus is like
- Temporal pattern
  - the spacing sequence of the electrical impulses

The Visual System
- Consists of the eyes, several parts of the brain and the pathways connecting them
- Retina
- Image forming system
  - cornea
  - pupil
  - lens
- Rods
- Cones
- Fovea

Seeing Light
- Sensitivity
- Dark adaptation
- Dark adaptation curve

Seeing Patterns
- Visual acuity
- Snellen acuity
- Contrast acuity

Seeing Color
- Converting wavelength into color
- Color constancy
- Color appearance
  - hue
  - brightness
  - saturation
- Color mixture
  - color-matching experiment
  - metamers
  - dichromats
  - monochromats

Theories of Color Vision
- Trichromacy theory
  - even though we can discriminate among many different colors, there are only three types of receptors for color
- Opponent-color theory
  - the theory that the visual system contains two types of color-sensitive units (Hering)

Hearing Key Concepts
- Sound waves
- Frequency
- Pitch
- Amplitude
- Loudness
- Decibel scale
- Timbre

The Auditory System
- Ears, parts of the brain and various connecting neural pathways
- Hearing system: transmission and transduction system
  - outer ear
  - middle ear
  - eardrum

Hearing Pitch Perception
- Temporal theory
- Resonance
- Place theory of pitch perception

Other Senses - Smell
- The olfactory system
- Olfactory bulb

Other Senses-Taste
- Taste receptors located on the tongue, throat and roof of the mouth
- Sensitivity to different taste stimuli vary from place to place on the tongue
- Sensitivity to salt, sweet, sour, bitter

Other Senses-Touch Pressure and Temperature
- Pressure
  - physical pressure on the skin
- Temperature
  - cold receptors and warm receptors

Pain
- Congenital insensitivity to pain
- The Pain system
  - variations in the quality of pain; phasic pain and tonic pain
- Nonstimulus determinants of pain
  - cultural considerations
- Acupuncture

Chapter 5: Perception

Perception
- How do organisms process and organize incoming raw sensory information in order to:
  - form a coherent representation or model of the world within which the organism lives?
  - use that representation to solve naturally occurring problems, such as navigating, grasping and planning?

Major Functions of the Perceptual System
- Determining which part of the sensory environment to attend to
- Localizing or determining where objects are
- Recognizing, determining what objects are
- Abstracting the critical information from objects
- Keeping the appearance of objects constant, even though their retinal images are changing

Selective Attention
- Screening or filtering information, selecting incoming information along various dimensions
- Eye movements
  - visual scanning
  - fixations
    - brief periods during which the eyes are relatively stationary and visual information is acquired from the environment
  - saccades
    - quick jumps of the eye from one place to the next during which vision is essentially suppressed

Selective Attention
- Weapon focus
  - research applied to armed crimes, where attention is primarily focused on the weapon
- Directed attention without eye movement
  - the ability to attend to visual stimulus without moving our eyes

_____

_____

_____

_____

_____

_____

_____

_____

_____

_____

_____

_____

_____

_____

_____

_____

_____

_____

_____

_____

_____

_____

_____

_____

_____

Auditory Attention
- Much of original research on attention done on auditory attention
- Multimodal
  - attention can move within a modality, such as from one visual stimulus to another, or between modalities, from seeing to listening

Attention, Perception and Memory
- Shadowing
  - repeating back one auditory message (we consciously remember little, if anything, about nonattended information)

Localization - Application
- Navigating around our environment
- Grasping an object
- Figure and ground
  - figure
    - the object of interest which appears more solid than the ground and appears in front of it
  - ground
    - the region that appears to be behind the figure

Grouping of Objects
- Grouping by proximity
  - if the vertical distance between two dots is reduced, columns will most likely be seen
- Grouping by similarity
  - grouping like objects with like objects

Perceiving Distance
- Depth cues
  - different kinds of visual information that, logically or mathematically, provide information about some object's depth
- Binocular cues
  - binocular disparity
- Monocular cues
  - relative size
  - interposition
  - relative height
  - perspective
  - shading and shadows
  - relative motion

Perceiving Motion
- Stroboscopic motion
- Real motion
- Selective adaptation
    - loss in sensitivity to motion is selective in that we lose sensitivity to the motion viewed and to similar motions, but not to motion that differs significantly in direction or speed

Recognition
- Determining where relevant objects are, and what they are
- Illusory conjunction
    - an incorrect combination of two separate attributes of an object
- Feature integration theory
    - primitive stage
        - qualities such as shape and color perceived (visual search task)
    - attentive stage
        - attention used to pull features together into an integrated whole

Feature Detection in the Cortex Key Concepts
- Pioneering research of Hubel and Wiesel (1968)
- Simple cells
    - respond when the eye is exposed to a line stimulus
- Complex cells
    - responds to a bar or edge in a particular orientation, but does not require that the stimulus be at a particular place within its receptive field
- Hypocomplex cells
    - require that the stimulus be in a particular orientation and also be of a particular length

Relations Among Features
- The relations among features must be specified/specifically aligned in order to achieve a result
- Gestalt psychologists
    - "the whole is more than the sum of its parts"

Later Stages of Recognition Network Models
- Simple networks (connectionist models)
  - the proposal that letters are described in terms of certain features, and that knowledge about what features go with what letter is contained in a network of connections

Networks with Feedback
- A letter is easier to perceive when it is presented as part of a word than when it is presented alone
- Top-down feedback connection
  - connections that go from the higher levels to the lower levels (explains why a letter is more perceptible when presented briefly in a word than when presented briefly alone)

Recognizing Natural Objects Features of Natural Objects
- Features must be capable of combining to form the shape of any recognizable object
- Must be such that they can be determined or constructed from more primitive features
- Geons
  - features and objects that include a number of geometric forms, such as cylinders, cones, blocks and wedges

The Importance of Context
- Distinction between bottom-up and top-down processing
- Bottom-up processing
  - driven solely by input, raw, sensory data
- Top-down processing
  - driven by a person's knowledge
- Ambiguous objects
  - objects that can be perceived in more than one way
- Effects of motives and desires on perception

Failure of Recognition
- Agnosia
  - breakdowns or disorders in recognition
- Associative agnosia
  - damage to the temporal lobe regions of the cortex that result in difficulty recognizing objects only when they are presented visually
- Prosopagnosia
  - category-specific deficits as a result of damage to the right hemisphere
- Pure alexia
  - the loss of the ability to recognize words as a result of damage to the left occipital lobe

Abstraction
- The process of reducing the vast amount of information that comes in from the physical world through our senses to a more manageable set of categories
- Abstracted information takes up less space and is therefore faster to work with than raw information

Constancy
- The brain's ability to maintain the perception of the underlying physical characteristics of an object, even when the sensory manifestations of the objects change drastically
- The major constancies are color (and brightness), shape, and size
- Constancies occur in all sensory modalities
- Various kinds of perceptual illusions can be explained by the perceptual system's insistence on maintaining constancies

The Neural Basis of Attention
- Two brain systems in attention
  - the posterior system
    - represents the perceptual features of an object, such as its location in space, its shape, color
  - the anterior system
    - designed to control when and how these features will be used for selection

- Visual cortex operates according to the principle of division of labor
- Recognition processes are subdivided into separate modules such as color, shape and texture

Perceptual Development
- Contributions of both nature and nurture
- Perceptual capacities of infants
  - preferential looking method
  - habituation method

Perception
- Perceiving forms
- Perceiving depth
- Perceiving constancies
- Controlled stimulation
  - absence of stimulation
  - limited stimulation
  - active perception

Chapter 6: Consciousness

Consciousness
- Current awareness of internal and external stimuli
- Monitoring ourselves and our environment
- Controlling ourselves and our environment

Preconscious Memories
- Memories that are accessible to consciousness
  - circadian rhythms
  - melatonin

The Unconscious
- Memories, impulses and desires that are not accessible to consciousness
- Freudian slips

Automaticity and Dissociation
- Automaticity – habitual actions and responses that do not require conscious attention
- Dissociation – thoughts and actions split off from rest of consciousness and function outside of awareness

Sleep and Dreams
- 5 Stages of sleep
- REM sleep; Non-REM (NREM) sleep

Sleep Theory
- Opponent-processing model
- Homeostatic sleep drive
- Clock-dependent alerting process

Sleep Disorders
- Sleep deprivation
- Insomnia
- Narcolepsy and apnea

Dreams
- Does everyone dream?
- How long do dreams last?
- Do people know when they are dreaming?
- Can people control the content of their dreams?

_____
_____
_____
_____
_____
_____
_____
_____
_____
_____
_____
_____
_____
_____
_____
_____
_____
_____
_____
_____
_____
_____
_____
_____

Theories of Dreaming
- Freudian theory
- Cognitive process
- Problem-solving function
- Day residue

Meditation
- Achieving an altered state of consciousness by performing certain rituals and exercises

Hypnosis
- An altered state of consciousness in which an individual relinquishes control over his/her behavior
- Hypnotic suggestions
- Posthypnotic amnesia
- Positive and negative hallucinations
- The hidden observer
- Hypnotherapy

Psychoactive Drugs
- Drugs that affect behavior, consciousness and/or mood
- Drug dependence
- Drug abuse

Categories of Drugs
- Depressants
- Opiates
- Stimulants
- Hallucinogens
- Cannabis

Psi Phenomena and Parapsychology
- Extrasensory perception (ESP)
  -telepathy
  -clairvoyance
  -precognition
- Psychokinesis

Chapter 7: Learning and Conditioning

Classical Conditioning: Key Terms and Concepts
- A learning process in which a previously neutral stimulus becomes associated with another stimulus through repeated pairing with that stimulus
- Leading theorist
  - Ivan Pavlov, Russian physiologist, early 20th century

Pavlov's Experiments: Key Terms and Concepts
- Unconditioned stimulus (UCS)
- Unconditioned response (UCR)
- Conditioned stimulus (CS)
- Conditioned response (CR)

Classical Conditioning
- Acquisition and Extinction
- Classical Conditioning in different species
- Second-order conditioning
- Generalization and Discrimination
- Inhibitory conditioning

Classical Conditioning Cognitive Factors
- Contiguity versus Predictability
- Predictability and Emotion

Classical Conditioning Biological Constraints
- Ethological Approach
  - emphasis on evolution and genetics
- Studies on taste aversion learning
  - different species learning the same thing by different means

Instrumental Learning: Key Terms and Concepts
- A learning process where certain responses are learned because they operate on, or affect, the environment
- Leading theorists
  - E. L. Thorndike, B. F. Skinner
- The law of effect (Thorndike)
  - responses that are followed by a positive consequence will be strengthened

Instrumental Learning: Key Terms and Concepts
- Reinforcement
  - process whereby the delivery of an appetitive stimulus or the removal of an aversive stimulus increases the probability of a behavior
- Positive reinforcement
  - describes a behavior that produces an appetitive stimulus
- Negative reinforcement
  - behavior prevents an aversive stimulus

Instrumental Learning: Key Terms and Concepts
- Punishment
  - the process by which delivery of an aversive stimulus or the removal of an appetitive stimulus decreases the probability of a behavior
- Omission training
  - behavior prevents an appetitive stimulus
- Implications for child rearing
- Shaping
  - reinforcing only variations in response that deviate in the direction desired by the experimenter

Applications
- Conditioned reinforcer: primary; secondary
- Generalization and discrimination
- Schedules of reinforcement
  - ratio schedules; fixed ratio; variable ratio
  - interval schedules; fixed interval; variable interval

Aversive Conditioning
- Punishment
  - a response is followed by an aversive stimulus or event, which results in the response being weakened or suppressed
- Escape and Avoidance
  - escape learning
  - avoidance learning

Control and Cognitive Factors
- Contingency versus Control
- Contingency Learning

Complex Learning

- Cognitive Maps and Abstract Concepts
  (Tolman)
- Cognitive map
  - the mental representation of the layout
    of a maze
- Insight Learning (Kohler)
- Prior Beliefs

Learning and Conditioning
- Habituation and Sensitization
- Phobias
- Eyeblink Conditioning
- Fear Conditioning

Chapter 8: Memory

Three Stages of Memory
- Encoding
  - when environmental information is translated into and stored as a meaningful entity
- Storage
  - when stored information is maintained over time
- Retrieval
  - when you attempt to pull from memory information that was previously encoded and stored

Three Memory Stores
- Memory processes differ between situations that require us to store material for:
  - less than a second
  - a matter of seconds
  - longer intervals from minutes to years
- The Atkinson-Shiffrin Theory proposes a distinction between different memories corresponding to different time intervals
  - sensory store
  - short-term store
  - rehearsal
  - elaboration
  - long-term store

Different Memories for Different Kinds of Information
- Explicit memory
  - a person consciously recollects an event as occurring in a particular time and place
- Implicit memory
  - a person unconsciously remembers information of various sorts

Sensory Memory
- Information initially acquired from the environment via the sense organs and placed into a short-lasting memory
- Iconic Memory
  - sensory memory corresponding to vision

_____
_____
_____
_____
_____
_____
_____
_____
_____
_____
_____
_____
_____
_____
_____
_____
_____
_____
_____
_____
_____
_____
_____
_____
_____
_____
_____
_____
_____

- Leading researcher
  - George Sperling (1960)
    - span of apprehension
    - partial-report procedure
    - whole-report condition
    - partial-report condition
    - auditory cue

Visible Persistence: The Temporal Integration Experiment
- Leading researchers
  - Di Lollo, Ericksen, Collins, Hogben
- Temporal-integration paradigm
  - 24 dots are presented in 24 of the 25 squares of an imaginary 5x5 array, and the observer's task is to report the location of the missing dot

Working Memory
- The information that is attended to (previously named short-term store)
- Involves encoding, storage and retrieval
- Phonological coding
  - for example, the sounds of the names of digits
- Visual coding
  - for example, the mental picture of digits
- Semantic coding
  - for example, based on some meaningful association that the digits have
- Used in solving various kinds of problems, such as mental arithmetic, geometric analogies and answering questions about text

Working Memory Systems
- Two distinct stores or buffers
  - Phonological buffer
    - stores information in an acoustic code
  - Spatial sketchpad
    - stores information in a visual or spatial code
- Working memory storage capacity is very limited (7 ± 2 items, or chunks
- Chunking
  - recoding new materials into larger, more meaningful units and storing those units in working memory

- Forgetting
  - decay of information over time, or displaced by new items

Retrieval

- Retrieval slows down as the number of items in working memory increases
- Sternberg memory-scanning task

Transfer from Working Memory to Long-term Memory

- Information may reside in working memory while it is being encoded or transferred into long-term memory
- Rehearsal
  - the conscious repetition of information in working memory
- Maintenance rehearsal
  - active efforts to hold information in working memory
- Elaborative rehearsal
  - efforts to encode information in long-term memory

Long-term Memory: Encoding

- Involved when information has to be retained for intervals as brief as a few minutes, or as long as a lifetime
- Encoding in long-term memory based on meaning and adding meaningful connections

Long-term Memory: Retrieval

- Forgetting the result of loss of access rather than loss of information (retrieval versus storage failure)
- Interference
  - if we associate different items with the same cue, when we try to use that cue to retrieve one of the items (the target item) the other items may become active and interfere with our recovery of the target

Interactions between Encoding and Retrieval

- Encoding factors that increase the chances of successful retrieval
  - organizing the information at the time of encoding
  - ensuring that the context in which information is encoded is similar to that in which it will be retrieved

Emotional Factors in Forgetting
- Emotion can influence long-term memory in five distinct ways
  - rehearsal
  - flashbulb memories
  - retrieval interference via anxiety
  - context effects
  - repression

Implicit and Explicit Memory
- Implicit memory refers to the kind of memory that manifests itself as an improvement on some perceptual, motor or cognitive task with no conscious recollection of the experiences that led to the improvement
- Explicit memory refers to the kind of memory manifested in recall or recognition when we consciously recollect the past

Implicit Memory
- Amnesia
  - partial loss of memory may result from injuries to the brain, strokes, electro convulsive shock, surgical procedures
- Anterograde Amnesia
  - profound inability to remember day to day events and acquire new factual information
- Retrograde Amnesia
  - an inability to remember events that occurred prior to the injury or disease
- Childhood Amnesia
  - an inability to recall events from the first years of life even through this is the time when experience is at its richest

Explicit Memory
- Episodic memory
  - refers to memory of personal episodes
- Semantic memory
  - refers to memory of facts and general truth

Constructive Memory
- Memory is a constructive and reconstructive process
  - the memory for an event can and does depart systematically from the objective reality that gave rise to it, both at the time it is formed (via constructive processes) and then later over time (via reconstructive memory)
- Constructive Perception
  - what is perceived forms the basis for the initial memory; therefore, if what is originally perceived differs systematically from the objective world, the perceiver's initial memory, and probably later memories as well, of what happened will likewise be distorted

Post-Event Memory Reconstruction
- We add new information to a memory that is suggested to us by others
- We change the memory when we revisit it in our minds
- We generate interferences and store these interferences as part of our memory
- We strip away information that does not seem to make sense in light of other facts we might know or have learned

Constructive Memory and the Legal System
- Eye-Witness Testimony
  - Confidence that his or her memory is accurate
- Important research findings influencing accuracy of memory
  - Original event causes poor encoding
    - poor lighting, lack of attention or any of a number of other factors
  - Some form of post event reconstruction
    - interferences or information suggested by others
  - Motivation and opportunity to rehearse the reconstructed memory

Constructive Memory and the Legal System
- Suggestive information and children's memories
- Forced confessions
- Jennifer Thompson's memory (case presentation at beginning of chapter)

Improving Memory
- Use of recoding schemes to enlarge the size of a chunk and thereby increase the memory span
- Improve encoding and retrieval by use of imagery, the basic principle underlying mnemonic systems such as the method of loci and the keyword method
- Improving encoding and retrieval by elaborating on the meaning of items and the way material is organized during encoding

Chapter 9: Language and Thought

Language Defined
- A multilevel system for relating thoughts to speech by means of words and sentence units

Language and Communication: Levels of Language
- Production
  - begins with thought
  - translated into a sentence
  - ends with sounds that express the sentence
- Comprehension
  - begins with hearing sounds
  - attaching meanings to the sounds in the form of words
  - combining the words to create a sentence
  - extract meaning from the sentence

Language Units and Processes
- Phoneme
  - a category of speech sounds. Every language has its own set of phonemes, with different sets for different languages, and rules for combining them into words
- Morpheme
  - the smallest unit of language that carries meaning. Most morphemes are words, but others are prefixes and suffixes that are added to words
- Syntactic rules are used for combining words into phrases and phrases into sentences
- The areas of the brain that mediates language lie in the left hemisphere and include Broca's area and Wernicke's area

The Development of Language
- Infants appear to be preprogrammed to learn phonemes, but need years to learn the rules
- Children learn words that name concepts familiar in their environment.
- Next children learn sentences, one word utterances, next telegraphic speech,and then elaborate their noun and verb phrases

- Children test hypotheses regarding critical utterances, such as word ends.
- Innate factors play a role; stage approach; critical period

Concepts and Categorization: The Building Blocks of Thought
- Propositional thought
  - the stream of sentences that we seem to "hear in our mind". Expresses a proposition or claim
- Imaginal thought
  - corresponds to images, particularly visual ones, that we can "see" in our minds
- Concept
  - represents an entire class; it is a set of properties that we associate with a particular class
- Categorization
  - the process of assigning an object to a concept
- Prototype
  - properties that describe the best examples of the concept

Concepts and Categorization
- Hierarchy of concepts
  - levels of categorization of objects, beginning at the basic level

Acquiring Concepts
- Learning prototypes and cores
  - explicit teaching, the means by which we learn cores and concepts
  - experience, the means by which we acquire prototypes
- Children often learn a new concept by using an exemplar strategy
  - a novel item is classified as an example of a concept if it is sufficiently similar to a known exemplar of the concept.
  - as children grow older, they also use hypothesis testing as a strategy for learning concepts
- Different neural regions may mediate different kinds of concepts and different categorization procedures

Reasoning
- Deductive reasoning
  - it is impossible for the conclusion of the argument to be false if its premises are true
- Heuristics
  - rules of thumb that operate on the content of propositions not on their logical form
- Inductive reasoning
  - it is improbable that the conclusion is false if the premises are true-reliance on similarity and causality heuristics
- Research on the neural bases of reasoning supports the distinction between deductive and inductive reasoning. Different parts of the brain become active when people evaluate deductive validity versus inductive strength

Imaginal Thought
- Thoughts that are manifested as visual images contain the kind of visual detail found in perception
- Mental images that are performed on Images, such as scanning and rotation are like those carried out on perceptions
- Imagery is like perceptions because both are mediated by the same parts of the brain.

Thought in Action: Problem Solving
- Difference reduction
  - setting up of subgoals, that when obtained, put us in a state closer to our goals
- Means-ends analysis
  - comparison of the current state to the goal state in order to find the most important differences between them and eliminating this difference becomes our main subgoal
- Work backward
  - reasoning from the goal to the subgoal, from that subgoal to another subgoal and so on
- Expert problem solvers differ from novices in four ways; more representations, apply solution principles, plan formation, forward reasoning

Chapter 10: Motivation

Motivation Defined
- A condition that energizes behavior and gives it direction
- Experienced subjects as a conscious desire
  - the desire for food, drink, sex

Motivation Theories
- Drive theories
  - emphasize the role of internal factors in motivation
- Incentive theory
  - emphasize the motivational role of external events or objects of desire
- Primary reinforcers
  - able to act as rewards independently of prior learning
- Secondary reinforcers
  - gained their status as rewards at least partially through learning about their relationship to other events

Reward and Incentive Motivation
- Incentive motivation
  - wanting something usually associated with affect
- Affect
  - refers to the entire range of consciously experienced pleasure and displeasure
- Wanting
  - the anticipation of pleasure
- Liking
  - the pleasure experienced in the moment
- Incentive salience
  - objects and events have become linked with anticipated affect

Drug Addiction and Reward
- Addiction
  - a pattern of compulsive and destructive drug-taking behavior
- Tolerance
  - the need for a greater amount of a drug to achieve the same euphoria
- Withdrawal
  - intensely aversive reaction to the cessation of drug use

Homeostasis and Drives
- Homeostasis
  - a constant internal state
- Set Point
  - the value that the homeostatic system tries to maintain
- Temperature and Homeostasis
- Thirst as a Homeostatic Process
  - the psychological manifestation of the need for water
  - extracellular thirst
  - intracellular thirst

Homeostasis and Drives
- Hunger
  - learning preferences
  - social learning mechanisms
  - conditioned aversion

Physiological Hunger Cues
- Peripheral signals
  - role of receptors in the stomach, intestine and liver
- Role of the brain - glucose - hypothalamus
  - lateral hypothalamus
  - ventromedial hypothalamus

Obesity Defined
- 30% or more in excess of one appropriate body weight
- Approximately 27% of Americans meet criteria

Factors Considered in the Study of Obesity
- Genetic factors
- Twin studies
- Fat cells
- Dieting and set point
- Overeating
- Breakdown of conscious restraints
- Emotional arousal
- Genetic factors
- Twin studies
- Dieting and weight control
- Weight control program

Anorexia and Bulimia
- Anorexia
  - an eating disorder characterized by extreme self-imposed weight loss at least 15% of the individual's minimum normal weight
- 20 times more likely to occur in women than in men, typically young women between teens and thirties
- Bulimia
  - an eating disorder characterized by recurrent episodes of binge eating (rapid consumption of a large amount of food in a discrete period of time) followed by attempts to purge the excess my means of vomiting or laxatives
- Typically affects young women
- Found among all racial, ethnic and socioeconomic groups

Sociocultural Causes
- Cultural emphasis on thinness in women
- Media images of the "ideal" female body
- Objectification theory
  - a sociocultural account of how being raised In a culture that sexually objectifies the female body alters girls and women's self-view and well-being
- Self-objectification
  - preoccupation with physical appearance characterized by vigilant appearance monitoring

Other Possible Causes of Anorexia
- Biological causes
  - hypothesis that anorexia is caused by malfunctions in the hypothalamus, the part of the brain that helps regulate eating
- Familial causes
  - family dynamics involving need for self-control and perfection, while suppressing expressions of warmth and conflict

Gender and Sexuality
- Distinction between adult sexuality and early sexual development
- Distinction between biological and environmental determinants of sexual behavior and feelings
- Debate over the role of biology, environment and learning in sexuality

Early Sexual Development
- Gender identity
  - males come to think of themselves as males and females as females
- Androgen
  - critical hormone in genital development
    - sufficient androgen – male genitals
    - insufficient androgen – female genitals
- Presence or absence of a male (Y) chromosome normally influences sexual development simply by determining whether the embryo will secrete androgens

Hormones vs. Environment
- Study of individuals exposed to prenatal hormones
- Exposure to anti-miscarriage drug, diethylstilbestrol, effects on gender identity
- Study of genetic males in Dominican Republic

Adult Sexuality
- Secretion of sex hormones called gonadotropins into the bloodstream
- Women
  - release of gonadotropins;
    - follicle-stimulating hormone (FSH)
    - luteinizing hormone (LH)
- Men
  - release of gonadotropins in a constant fashion rather than in a monthly cycle
    - interstitial cell stimulating hormone (ICSH)

Effects of Hormones on Desire and Arousal
- Effects of gonad removal
  - gonadectomy
- Removal of the testes
  - castration

- Relationship between hormonal fluctuation and sexual desire
- Studies of premenopausal and postmenopausal women

Neural Controls
- Role of hypothalamus in sexual behavior
- Stimulation of brain regions near hypothalamus reported to induce intense sexual feelings

Early Experiences
- Play behavior in mammals
- Importance of proximity and affectional bonds

Cultural Influences
- Influence of culture on sexual desire and human sexual behavior
- Varying degrees of permissiveness and restrictions on sexual activity including, sexual activity among children, homosexuality, masturbation and premarital intercourse

Sexual Differences
- Gender differences in attitudes about sex, including views on emotional or sexual infidelity
- Gender differences in patterns of sexual behavior

Sexual Orientation
- The degree to which an individual is sexually attracted to persons of the same or opposite sex
- Pioneering research of Alfred Kinsey

Causes of Sexual Orientation
- Nature - Nurture question
- Research findings on gender nonconformity (Bell, Weinberg, Hammersmith) (1981)

Chapter 11: Emotion

Emotion Defined
- A complex, multicomponent episode that created a readiness to act
- Six components of emotion
  - cognitive appraisal
  - subjective experience
  - thought and action tendencies
  - internal bodily reactions
  - facial expression
  - responses to emotions

Cognitive Appraisal and Emotion
- The interpretation of the person/environment relationship
  - responsible for differentiating the emotions

Classic Theories of Emotion
- Two-factor theory
  - leading theorists, Schacter and Singer
- James-Lange theory
- Facial-feedback hypothesis

Themes and Dimensions of Appraisal (Additional Theories)
- Minimalist appraisal theories (core relational theme)
- Dimensional appraisal theories
- Conscious and unconscious appraisal

Appraisal in the Brain: Key Brain Structure
- Amygdala
  - small almond-shaped mass located in the lower brain and known to register emotional reactions

Subjective Experiences and Emotion
- Thought and action tendencies
  - urges in behavior that accompany emotions

Feelings Modify Attention and Learning
- We tend to pay more attention to events that fit our current feelings than to events that do not
- Important research in this area
  - Bower (1981)
  - Derryberry and Tucker (1994)

Feelings Modify Evaluations and Judgments
- Our feelings can affect our evaluation of other people
- Important research in this area
  - Isen, Shalker, Clark and Karp (1978)
  - Lerner, Keltner (2001)
  - Siemer (2001)

Bodily Changes and Emotion
- Role of the sympathetic nervous system as the body is prepared for emergency action
- Role of the parasympathetic nervous system in calming the body and conserving energy
- Undoing effect of positive emotions
  - helps people recover from lingering arousal that follows negative emotions

Intensity of Emotions
- Visceral perception
  - the perception of our own arousal
- Important research in this area
  - army veterans with spinal cord injuries; Hohmann (1962)

Differentiation of Emotions
- Do the patterns of physiological activity differ for different emotions?
- James-Lange theory
  - different autonomic arousal for different emotions
- Walter Cannon theory
  - denies that autonomic arousal can differentiate emotions

Facial Expression and Emotion
- Universal meaning of certain facial expressions
- Emotional display rules
  - specify the types of emotions people should express in certain situations and the behaviors appropriate for particular emotions
- Facial-feedback hypothesis
  - we receive feedback from our autonomic arousal as well as from our facial expression

Emotional Regulation
- People's responses to their own emotions
- Strategies employed to regulate or control emotions

Emotions, Gender and Culture
- Gender differences in the expression of emotion rather than in the experience of emotion
- Cultural differences
  - role of collectivism and/or individualism on emotion

Aggression
- Behavior intended to injure another person (physically or verbally) or to destroy property
- Frustration-aggression hypothesis
  - when a person's effort to reach a goal is blocked, an aggressive drive is induced

Aggression as a Learned Response
- Social-learning theory
  - principles of reinforcement and role of cognitive processes
- Vicarious learning
  - learning by observation

Aggressive Expression and Catharsis
- Catharsis or purging an emotion by experiencing it intensely
- Research on media violence

Chapter 12: Intelligence

Assessment of Intellectual Abilities
- Reliability
  - reproducible and consistent results
    - internal reliability
    - interrater reliability
- Validity
  - measures what it is intended to measure
    - criterion or empirical validity
    - construct validity
- Standardization
  - conditions are the same for all the test takers

Early Intelligence Tests
- Sir Francis Galton
- Alfred Binet
- Stanford-Binet Intelligence Scale (Lewis Terman)
  - intelligence quotient (IQ); expression of intelligence as a ratio of mental age to chronological age IQ =MA/CA*100
- Wechsler Intelligence Scales (WAIS)
  - verbal scale
  - performance scale

Group Administered General Abilities Tests
- The Scholastic Assessment Test (SAT)
- The American College Test (ACT)

Cultural Considerations
- Concerns of bias in favor of middle and upper-class Europeans against cultural minorities

Contemporary Theories of Intelligence
- Information processing approach
- Gardner's theory of Multiple Intelligences (7 distinct kinds of intelligence)
  - linguistic
  - musical
  - logical - mathematical
  - spatial
  - bodily - kinesthetic
  - intrapersonal
  - interpersonal

Anderson's Theory of Intelligence and Cognitive Development
- Differences in intelligence result from differences in "basic processing mechanism".
- Individuals vary in speed at which basic processing occurs

Sternberg's Triachic Theory
- Three parts or subtheories
  - component subtheory
  - experiential subtheory
  - contextual subtheory

Ceci's Bioecological Theory
- Proposes that there are "multiple cognitive potentials" that are biologically based, and shaped by the individual's environment

Cross-cultural Perspectives on Intelligence
- Emphasis on social intelligence, social competence and self-knowledge

Genetics and Intelligence
- Debates over the contribution of genetics to determine levels of intelligence
- Heritability
  - the percentage of variance in any trait that is accounted for by genetic differences among the individuals
- Misunderstandings about heritability

Chapter 13: Personality

Personality Defined
- The distinctive and characteristic patterns of thought, emotion and behavior that make up an individual's personal style of interacting with the physical and social environment

Personality Factors
- Research of British psychologist Hans Eysenck
- Introversion – extraversion
- Emotional instability – stability

Five Traits Factors
- Consensus among researchers that 5 trait dimensions capture most of what we mean by personality – referred to as the "Big Five"

Personality Inventories
- Questionnaires that assess personality
- Minnoseta Multiphasic Personality Inventory (MMPI)
  - criterion: keyed method or empirical construction
  - first major inventory to incorporate a number or validity scales within it
- Q-Sought: a rater or sorter describes an individual's personality by sorting a set of approximately 100 cards into piles

Personality: The Psychoanalytic Approach
- Theoretical Approach created by Sigmund Freud
- Role of unconscious processes in behavior
- Free association
- Psychological Determinism
  - All thoughts, emotions and actions have causes

Personality Structure: The Psychoanalytic Approach
- The ID
  - Most primitive part of personality and the part from which the ego and the superego later develop
- The Ego
  - Obeys the reality principle; the gratification of impulses must be delayed until the situation is appropriate
- The Superego
  - The moral judge of whether actions are right or wrong

Personality Dynamics: The Psychoanalytic Approach
- Conservation of energy
  - libido or psychic energy
- Anxiety and Defense
  - defense mechanisms or strategies for reducing or preventing anxiety
- Defense Mechanisms
  - Repression
  - Rationalization
  - Reaction Formation
  - Projection
  - Intellectualization
  - Denial
  - Displacement

Modification of Freud's Theories Neo-Freudians
- Modified or dissented from Freud's theory of personality
  - Carl Jung
  - Alfred Adler
  - Karen Horney
  - Harry Stack Sullivan
  - Erich Fromm

Personality Test
- Projective tests
  - Rorschach
    - series of 10 cards displaying complex ink blots
  - Thematic Apperception Test (TAT)
    - 20 ambiguous pictures of persons and scenes from which the individual is asked to tell a story

Personality: The Behaviorist Approach
- Emphasizes the importance of environmental or situational determinants of behavior
- Behavior is the result of a continuous interaction between personal and environmental variables
- Places little emphasis on individual differences

The Behaviorist Approach: Social Learning and Conditioning
- Operant conditioning
  - the type of learning that occurs when our behavior is based on reinforcement or punishment
- Observational learning
  - learning by observing the actions of others and noting the consequences of those actions
- Classical Conditioning
  - the type of learning that occurs when specific situations become associated with specific outcomes

Personality: The Cognitive Approach
- Emphasizes how people process information about themselves and the world
- Individual differences in the way people mentally represent information

Personality: Social Learning Approach
- Leading theorists
  - Albert Bandura, Walter Mischel
- Internal cognitive processes influence behavior as well as observations of the behavior of others and the environment in which behavior occurs
- Social cognitive theory
  - Reciprocal determinism: external determinants of behavior (rewards, punishment) and internal determinants (beliefs, thoughts, expectations) are part of a system of interacting influences that effect behavior and other parts of the system

Personality: Kelly's Personal Construct Theory
- Leading theorist
  - George Kelly
- Goal is to discover personal constructs, the dimensions that individuals themselves use to interpret themselves and their social world

Personality: Self - Schemas
- A schema is a cognitive construct that helps us perceive, organize, process and utilize information
- Relatively stable over time
- Individual differences in schemas and therefore individual differences in processing information

Personality: The Humanistic Approach
- Leading theorist
  - Carl Rogers
- Actualizing tendency
  - a tendency toward fulfillment or actualization of all the capacities of the individual
- The Self
  - consists of all the ideas, perceptions and values that characterize "I" or "me"
- Unconditional Positive Regard
  - being given the sense that one is valued by parents and others even when feelings, attitudes and behaviors are less than ideal

Personality: The Humanistic Approach
- Leading theorist
  - Abraham Maslow
- Hierarchy of Needs
  - the needs at one level must be at least partially satisfied before those at the next level become important motivators of action

Personality: The Evolutionary Approach
- Leading theorists
  - David Buss , Douglass Kenrick
- Behaviors that increased the organism's chances of surviving and leaving descendants will be selected over evolutionary history and become aspects of humans' personalities
- Focus on mate selection, reproductive and mating strategies

The Genetics of Personality
- Personality traits are largely determined by the genes an individual was born with
- Twin Studies

Interactions Between Personality and Environment
- Genotype environment correlation
- Reactive Interaction
- Evocative Interaction
- Proactive Interaction

_____

_____

_____

_____

_____

_____

_____

_____

_____

_____

_____

_____

_____

_____

_____

_____

_____

_____

_____

_____

_____

_____

_____

_____

_____

Chapter 14: Stress, Health, and Coping

Stress, Health and Coping: Key Terms and Definitions
- Stress
  - experiencing events that are perceived as endangering one's physical or psychological well-being
- Stressor
  - the events themselves
- Stress responses
  - the reaction to the events
- Behavioral medicine
  - the study of how stress and other social, psychological and biological factors come together to contribute to illness

Categories of Stressful Events
- Traumatic events
- Uncontrollable events
- Unpredictable events
- Events that challenge the limits of our capabilities and self-concept

Traumatic Events
- Situations of extreme danger that are outside the range of usual human experience
- Traumatic events examples:
  - war
  - car or plane crashes
  - physical assault

Psychological Reactions to Traumatic Events
- Unaware of injuries
- Disoriented
- Readily compliant
- Anxiety
- Apprehension
- Difficulty concentrating

Controllability of an Event
- The degree to which we can stop an event or bring it about
- The more uncontrollable an event seems, the more likely it is to be perceived as stressful
- Important role of perception in our assessment of controllability of stressful events

_____
_____
_____
_____
_____
_____
_____
_____
_____
_____
_____
_____
_____
_____
_____
_____
_____
_____
_____
_____

Predictability of an Event
- The degree to which we know if and when an event will occur
- Research findings on predictability of events, emotional arousal and stress

Stressful Life Events
- Life changes, both positive and negative that require numerous readjustments
- Research findings of Holmes and Rahe (1967)

Internal Conflicts
- Unresolved issues that may be either conscious or unconscious
- Conflicts may arise when two inner needs or motives are in opposition
  - independence versus dependence
  - intimacy versus isolation
  - cooperation versus competition
  - expressions of impulses versus moral standards

Psychological Reactions to Stress
- Anxiety
- Anger and aggression
- Apathy and depression
- Cognitive impairment

Psychological Reactions to Stress
Post-Traumatic Stress Disorder (PTSD)
- Symptoms of PTSD:
  - detachment from everyday life
  - repeated reliving of the trauma
  - sleep disturbances
  - survivor guilt

Physiological Reactions to Stress
- Increased metabolic rate
- Increased heart rate
- Dilation of pupils
- Higher blood pressure
- Increased breathing rate
- Tensing of muscles
- Secretion of endorphins and ACTH
- Release of extra sugar from the liver

The General Adaptation Syndrome
- A set of responses that is displayed by all organisms in response to stress
  - Alarm
    - body mobilizes to confront a threat
  - Resistance
    - the organism attempts to cope with the threat by fleeing it or fighting it
  - Exhaustion
    - the organism may deplete its physiological resources

How Stress Affects Health
- Psychophysiology Disorders
  - physical disorders in which emotions are believed to play a central role
    - coronary heart disease
    - the immune system
    - health-related behaviors

Psychological Factors and Stress Responses
- Psychoanalytic theory
  - neurotic anxiety; anxiety out of proportion to the actual danger and which stems from unconscious conflicts between unacceptable impulses and the constraints imposed by reality

Psychological Factors and Stress Responses
- Behavioral theory
  - learned behavior, in which individuals learn to associate stress responses with certain situations.

Psychological Factors and Stress Responses
- Cognitive theory
  - attributions or causal explanations people give for important events
- Attributional styles
  - internal/external
  - stable/unstable
  - global/specific
- Optimism/Pessimism

Hardiness
- Focuses on people who are most resistant to stress, who do not become physically or emotionally impaired even in the face of major stressful events

Finding Meaning
- Focuses on people who, when confronted with a major trauma say that they feel their lives have changed in extremely positive ways as a result of their experiences

Type A Behavior
- Describes people who exhibit a behavior pattern that is extremely competitive and achievement oriented; they have a sense of time urgency, find it difficult to relax, and become impatient and angry when confronted with delays or with people who they view as incompetent

Coping Skills
- Coping refers to the process by which a person attempts to manage stressful demands
  - problem-focused coping: focuses on the specific problem or situation, trying to find ways of changing it or avoiding it in the future
  - emotion-focused coping: focuses on alleviating the emotions associated with the stressful situation, even if the situation itself cannot be changed

Managing Stress
- Behavioral Techniques
  - biofeedback
  - relaxation training
  - meditation
  - aerobic exercise

Managing Stress
- Cognitive Techniques: changing the individuals cognitive responses to stressful situations
  - cognitive behavior therapy attempts to help people identify the kinds of stressful situations that produce their physiological or emotional symptoms and alter the way they cope with these situations

Chapter 15: Abnormal Psychology

Abnormality Defined
- Deviation from cultural norms
- Deviation from statistical norms
- Maladaptive behavior
- Personal distress

Defining Abnormality
- Appropriate perceptions of reality
- Ability to exercise voluntary control over behavior
- Self-esteem and acceptance
- Ability to form affectionate relationships
- Productivity

Classifying Abnormal Behavior
- Classification system
- DSM-IV

Perspectives on Mental Disorders
- Biological perspective
  - medical or disease model
- Psychological perspective
  - psychoanalytic
  - behavioral
  - cognitive
- Cultural or sociological perspectives

Anxiety Disorders
- A group of disorders in which anxiety either is the main symptom or is experienced when the individual attempts to control certain maladaptive behaviors.

Anxiety Disorders
- Generalized anxiety disorder
- Panic disorders
  - with agoraphobia
  - without agoraphobia
- Phobias
  - an intense fear of a stimulus or situation that most people do not consider particularly dangerous
    - simple phobias
    - social phobias

Obsessive-Compulsive Disorders
- Repetitive acts of thoughts
- Obsessions
  - persistent intrusions of unwelcome thoughts, images, or impulses that elicit anxiety
- Compulsions
  - irresistible urges to carry out certain acts or rituals that reduce anxiety

Mood Disorders
- Depressive disorders
- Bipolar disorders
- Depression
  - Symptoms manifested in several domains
    - emotional
    - cognitive
    - motivational
    - physical
- Bipolar disorder
  - Manic episodes
    - energetic
    - enthusiastic
    - full of self confidence
    - little need of sleep
    - grandiose plans
- Biological perspective
  - genetic component
  - neurotransmitters: serotonin, norepinephrine

Mood Disorders
- Cognitive perspective
  - interpretation of events
  - cognitive triad – Aaron Beck
  - attributional style – Martin Seligman

Mood Disorders
- Psychoanalytic perspective
  - early childhood experiences of loss of parental affection
  - overdependence on external approval
  - internalization of anger

Schizophrenia: Major Characteristics
- Delusions
  - disturbances in thought and attention
- Hallucinations
  - disturbances in perception
- Disturbances in emotional expression
- Decreased ability to function

Schizophrenia: Biological Perspective
- Hereditary predisposition
- Structural deficits
  - prefrontal cortex
  - enlarged ventricles
  - neurotransmitter dopamine

Schizophrenia: Social and Psychological Perspectives
- Stress
- High expressed emotion
- Cultural differences

Personality Disorders
- Enduring ways of perceiving or relating to the environment and thinking about oneself.
- Longstanding patterns of maladaptive behavior
- Immature and inappropriate ways of coping with stress and solving problems
- Usually evident in early adolescence and may continue throughout the lifespan and across situations
- Persons with personality disorders often so not feel upset or anxious about their behavior and may not be motivated to change their behavior

Antisocial Personality Disorder
Defining Characteristics
- Little sense of responsibility, morality or concern for others
- Behavior determined almost entirely by own needs and desires
- Seek immediate gratification of needs and cannot tolerate frustration
- Great facility for lying and need for thrills and excitement, with little concern for possible injury
- More commonly diagnosed in men

Antisocial Personality Disorder: Biological Determinants
- Role of genetics – twin studies, adoption studies
- Role of neurotransmitters – serotonin
- Structure and functioning of parts of the brain
- Deficits in ability to sustain concentration, in reasoning, self-monitoring and self-awareness
- Differences in levels of arousability

Antisocial Personality Disorder:
Social Factors
- Role of family and parenting
  - parental non-involvement, children frequently unsupervised
  - hostility of parents toward children
- Interaction of biological and family factors
  - neuropsychological problems, the result of maternal drug use, child abuse, birth complications, coupled with poor parenting

Antisocial Personality Disorder:
Personality Factors
- Information processing about social interactions
- Actions of others seen as aggressive rather than accidental
- Responses other than aggression seen as ineffective

Borderline Personality Disorder:
Defining Characteristics
- Extreme variability and instability in mood, relationships and self-perception
- Bouts of severe depression, anxiety and anger
- Periods of extreme self-doubt and grandiose self-importance
- Periods of extreme dependency and emotional vulnerability
- Self-mutilation, burning or cutting
- Comorbid disorders include substance abuse, depression, generalized anxiety disorder, panic disorder
- History of marital and employment difficulties
- More commonly diagnosed in women

Borderline Personality Disorder:
Psychoanalytic Explanations
- Reliance on primitive defense mechanisms
- Often history of abuse
- Poorly developed view of self and others
- Shifting concepts between "all good" or "all bad"

Dissociative Identity Disorder:
Defining Characteristics
(formerly Multiple Personality Disorder)

- A single individual of two or more distinct identities or personalities
- Described as a failure to integrate various aspects of identity, memory and consciousness
- Identities alternate in controlling behavior
- Primary identity has no awareness of the experienced of the other identities
- Periods of unexplained amnesia
- History of physical and sexual abuse
- Enhanced susceptibility to self-hypnosis
- Increase in reported cases of DID in United States

Insanity As A Legal Defense

- M'Naghten Rule
- American Law Institute Rule
- Guilty but mentally ill

Chapter 16: Treatment of Psychological Disorders

Historical Background:
Beliefs and Treatment of Mentally Ill
Beliefs
- Possession by evil spirits and demons
- Lack of balance between positive and negative energies
- Disturbance in the balance of bodily fluids treatment

Treatment
- Demons exorcised through prayer, magic incantation
- Mentally ill beaten and treated like animals, tortured, starved and sentenced to death
- Greek physician Hippocrates credited with more humane treatment of mentally ill, who were placed in pleasant surroundings, given soothing baths, massages
- Interventions of Philippe Pinel removed restraints and treated mentally ill more humanely

Modern Treatment Facilities
- Hospitalization
- Community Mental Health Centers
  - Advances in psychotropic medication
  - Deinstitutionalization
  - Consequences of deinstitutionalization

Psychotherapy Settings
- Hospitals
- Community Mental Health Centers
- Private offices

Professionals Who Provide Psychotherapy
- Psychiatrists
- Psychoanalysts
- Psychologists
  - clinical
  - counseling
  - school
- Psychiatric social workers

Techniques of Psychotherapy
- Psychodynamic therapy
  - free association
  - dream analysis
  - transference

Techniques of Psychotherapy
- Behavior therapy
  - principles of learning, conditioning, reinforcement
  - systematic desensitization
  - in-vivo exposure
  - selective reinforcement
  - modeling
  - behavioral rehearsal
  - self-regulation

Techniques of Psychotherapy
- Cognitive-behavior therapy
  - behavior modification plus a focus on changing reasoning and thinking

Applications of Cognitive-Behavior Therapy
- Anxiety disorders
- Depression
- Eating Disorders
- Drug and Alcohol Dependence
- Sexual Dysfunction

Techniques of Psychotherapy
- Humanistic Therapies
  - emphasizes individual tendency toward growth and self-actualization
  - Carl Rogers; Client-centered therapy
  - empathy, warmth, genuineness

Sociocultural Approaches
- Group therapy
- Self-help groups
- Marital and family therapy
- Community based programs

Culturally Specific Therapy
- Different forms of therapy might be more acceptable to members of specific ethnic groups.
- Matching clients and therapists from same culture and gender
- Sensitivity to the influences of culture and gender on clients attitude toward therapy

Eclectic Approaches
- Use of a combination of approaches and techniques from different therapies

Special Issues in Treating Children
- Effectiveness of types of therapy depends on type of disorder
- Concerns around development levels
- Family dynamics must be addressed
- Level of motivation affected by the fact that most children do not initiate treatment for themselves

Effectiveness of Psychotherapy
- How effective
- Which methods most effective

Evaluating Psychotherapy
- Spontaneous remission
  - ethical considerations
- Outcome measures
  - client's evaluation
  - therapist's evaluation
  - third party, ex. family or other clinician
  - research finding of Hans Eysenck

Comparing Therapies
- Research findings
- Difficulties encountered in comparing therapies

Common Factors in Psychotherapy
- Quality of interpersonal relationship between client and therapist
- Desensitization to problems
- Reinforcement of adaptive responses
- Understanding and insight

Biological Therapies
- Use of electroconvulsive shock
- Psychotherapeutic drugs

Electroconvulsive Therapy (ECT)
- Electric current applied to the brain
- Controversial history
- Side effects of ECT

Combining Biological and Psychological Approaches in the Treatment of Psychological Disorders
- Depression
- Anxiety
- Schizophrenia

Effects of Culture and Gender on Psychotherapy
- Diagnosis
- Willingness to seek and remain in therapy
- Type of therapy
- Rates of hospitalization

Enhancing Mental Health
- Monitor feelings and behavior
- Analyze motives and abilities
- Accept feelings
- Know vulnerabilities
- Develop talents and interests
- Become involved with other people
- Know when to seek help

Cutting Edge Research: Herbal Treatments For Mental Disorders
- St. John's Wort - depression
- Valerian, Kava – anxiety
- Gingko biloba – memory

Chapter 17: Social Influence

Social Psychology Defined
- The scientific study of the ways that people's behavior and mental processes are shaped by the real or imagined presence of others

Social Psychology: Key Concepts
- Fundamental attribution error
  - the tendency to explain other people's actions by overestimating character and underestimating the influence of situations or circumstances
- Social facilitation
  - the boosting effects of the presence of someone else doing the same task
- Social inhibition
  - the derailing effect or tendency to decrease performance in the presence of others
- Stroop task
  - a complex task, where a person is asked to identify the ink color in which words or symbols are printed
- Stroop interference
  - the difficulty in following instruction to ignore the printed word and name the word's ink color

Deindividuation
- Certain group situations can minimize the salience of people's personal identities, reduce their sense of public accountability, and in doing so produce aggressive or unusual behavior
- Key characteristics that contribute to deindividuation
  - group size
  - anonymity

Bystander Effects
- People are less likely to help when others are present
- Pluralistic ignorance
  - everybody in the group misleads everybody else by defining the situation as a non-emergency

- Diffusion of responsibility
  - when each individual knows that many others are present, the burden of responsibility does not fall on one person

Bystander Effect

- Role of helping models
  - individuals use other people as models to define a situation and decide when to be helpful
- Role of information
  - information about social psychological phenomena can lessen the power that situations have to influence behavior

Compliance and Obedience

- Leading researcher
  - Solomon Asch
- Classic study on compliance (1952, 1955, 1958)
- Important findings
  - the pressure to conform is far less strong when the group is not unanimous

Social Influences and Conformity

- Informational social influence
  - we conform because we believe that other people's interpretations of an ambiguous situation are more correct than our own
- Nominative social influence
  - we conform to a group's social norms or typical behavior to become liked and accepted

Minority Influence

- The finding that minorities can move or change minorities toward their point of view if they present a consistent position without appearing rigid, dogmatic, or arrogant

Obedience to Authority

- Leading research
  - Stanley Milgram, Yale University
- Important findings
  - 65% of participants in the study obeyed request to administer a series of potentially harmful electrical shocks

Influences on Rates of Obedience
- Surveillance
  - diminished surveillance, decreases obedience
- Buffers
  - proximity and psychological distance. The more direct the participants' experience with the victim, the less the participant will obey

Influences on Rates of Obedience
- Role models
  - the more role models who disobeyed, the more likely for the participant to also disobey
- Emerging situations
  - when the situation starts out as innocuous and changes rapidly, this influences the likelihood of the participant to obey
- Ideology
  - a set of beliefs and attitudes that legitimizes the authority of the person in charge and justifies following his or her directions

Ethical Issues
- Criticisms of Milgram's Study
  - deception
  - debriefing

Obedience in Everyday Life
- Leading researchers
  - Hofling, Brotzman et al. 1966
- Application to hospital rules, professional practice

Internalization
- Attempts to change private attitudes, not just public behaviors and to obtain changes that will be sustained over time
- Self-justification
  - pressure to be consistent can be so strong, that people will rationalize past behavior by adjusting their private beliefs to support it.
- Foot-in-the-door technique
  - people will say yes to requests that would ordinarily lead to no, if initially a small request is made, that few should refuse

Cognitive Dissonance Theory
- Leading theorist
  - Leon Festinger
- There is a drive toward cognitive consistency which motivates the person to remove the discomfort and bring the cognitions into harmony

Self-Perception Theory
- Leading theorist
  - Daryl Bem
- Individuals know their own attitudes, emotions and internal states based on observations of their own behavior and circumstances in which the behavior occurs
- Overjustification Effort
  - people go overboard and explain their own behavior with too much emphasis on situational causes and not enough on personal causes

Reference Groups and Identification
- Identification
  - adopting beliefs of individuals or groups obeying norms in order to be like them or to identify with them
- Reference group
  - groups with which we identify and use to evaluate and regulate our opinions and actions

Group Interactions
- Institutional norms
  - implicit or explicit rules of acceptable behavior and beliefs applied to entire institutions or organizations, example schools, prisons, governments
- Leading research
  - Philip Zimbardo's Stanford Prison Experiment

Group Decision Making
- Group Polarization
  - group decisions are more extreme than would be individual decisions
- Group Think
  - members of a group suppress their own opinions or feelings of dissent and go along with the group decision

Chapter 18: Social Cognition

Social Cognition Defined
- Examines people's subjective interpretations of their social experiences as well as their modes of thinking about the social world

Social Cognition: Key Concepts
- Schematic Processing
  - the process of searching in the memory for the schema that is most consistent with the incoming data
- Stereotypes
  - schemas for classes or subtypes of people
- Self-schemas
  - schemas about ourselves, a set of organized self-concepts stored in memory
- Priming
  - Incidental activation of schemas by situational concepts
- Primary effect
  - the first information we receive has the greater impact on our overall impressions
- Inferences
  - judgments that go beyond the information given
- Self-fulfilling prophecy
  - stereotypes that can set in motion a chain of behavioral processes that serve to draw out from others behavior that confirms the initial stereotype
- Stereotype threat
  - the mere threat of being identified with a stereotype can raise an individual's anxiety level, which in turn degrades his or her performance
- Individuation
  - assessing an individual's personal qualities on a person-by-person basis

Overcoming Stereotypes
- Be aware of the potential negative influences of stereotypes
- Be motivated to reduce prejudice
- Engage in controlled and deliberate thinking

Attributions

- Intuitive attempts to infer the causes of behavior
- Dispositional attribution
  - an inference that something about the person is primarily responsible for the behavior
- Situational attribution
  - an inference that something internal is primarily responsible for the behavior (Ex: money, social norms)
- Fundamental attribution error
  - we underestimate the situational influences on behavior and assume that some personal characteristic of the individual is responsible

Attitudes

- Likes and dislikes
  - favorable or unfavorable evaluations of and reactions to objects, people, situations, or other aspects of the world

Persuasive Communication

- Elaboration likelihood model
  - aims to predict when certain aspects of persuasive communication will matter and when it won't
- The central route to persuasion
  - applies when an individual mentally responds to and elaborates on the persuasive communication
- The peripheral route to persuasion
  - applies when an individual responds to non-content cues in a communication or to the context of the communication

Attitudes and Behavior

- Assumption that a person's attitudes determine his or her behavior
- Attitudes appear to predict behavior under the following conditions:
  - attitudes are strong and consistent
  - attitudes are specifically related to the behavior being predicted
  - attitudes are based on direct experience
  - the individual is aware of his or her attitude

Interpersonal Attraction

- Liking and Attraction
  - physical attractiveness
  - proximity
  - familiarity
  - similarity
  - transference
- Loving and Mating
  - love and Marriage
  - love of Self - expansion - increase in our potential abilities and resources
  - passionate Love
  - companionate Love

The Triangular Theory of Love

- Intimacy
  - emotional component
- Passion
  - sexual attraction and romantic feelings
- Commitment
  - intention to remain in the relationship